THE DREAM OF VIXEN TOR

A Restoring the Crown Book

THE DREAM OF VIXEN TOR

Ken Eagle Feather

Illustrations by Charles Duffie
Poems by Harriet Louisa Coleman

Cover and interior design by Charles Duffie

Published by Tracker One Studios, Inc.
P.O. Box 4608 Charlottesville, VA 22905
www.trackerone.com

Distributed by Hampton Roads Publishing Co., Inc.
1125 Stoney Ridge Road, Charlottesville, VA 22902
Phone (804) 296-2772 | Fax: (804) 296-5096
hrpc@hrpub.com | www.hrpub.com

If you are unable to order this book from your
local bookseller, you may order directly from the
distributor. Call toll-free 800-766-8009.

Library of Congress Card Number: 00-105410

ISBN 0-9701506-0-1
10 9 8 7 6 5 4 3 2 1

Printed on acid-free paper in China

DEDICATION

To the joy of my heart,
my lovely daughter, Emma.
Ken Eagle Feather

To Genevieve, in remembrance of Dakota
winters, Yosemite summers, and all the roads
and rest stops we've seen these twenty years.
Charles Duffie

I'd like to dedicate this lovely book to Wanda
Hrynash because she is a really good friend to me,
and when I see her she makes me happy.
Harriet Louisa Coleman

CONTENTS

THE DREAM OF VIXEN TOR

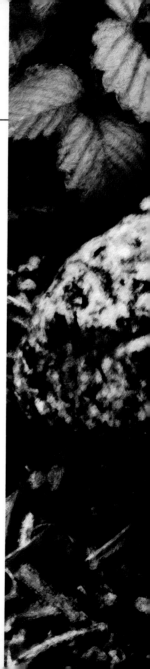

Vixen Tor
Silent at night foxes come leaping
across the hill tops, sniffing their prey
away, away.
Whispers of the moon cry,
shining brightly,
reflecting on the fairys' pond
in the lavender field.
Stars come and go
passing their lives in five seconds.

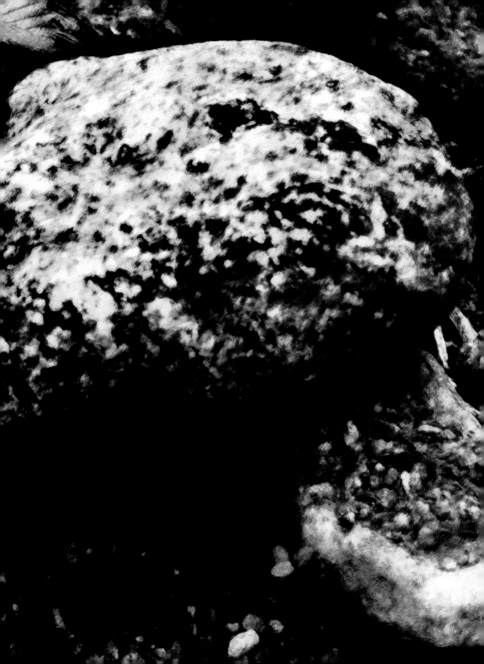

After the passing of King Arthur, the lessons of the crown slipped uneasily into disarray. Arthur's subjects had lost their sense of nation and self, and floundered amidst feelings of having no direction to travel. Even with the prosperity of his legacy, it was a time of great confusion and despair.

It was Arthur's last request to the Knights of the Round Table (the most able of men, who had gathered simply to share one of the greatest adventures ever known) that before they dispersed to the four winds, they train a special breed of men and women, beginning a longstanding lineage of trackers and travelers known as rangers.

It was to the rangers that the task of restoring the crown—of restoring the relationship of the people to the spirit of all things good and whole, and to the spirit that contained all worlds—fell. Merlin, adviser to King Arthur and one of the greatest wizards ever born, was even thought to have participated in this training, as the quest for freedom was firmly fixed within his heart as well.

This, then, is the story of one of those rangers trained by the bold dreams of King Arthur's knights and, yes, of Merlin, himself. It also begins the story of a gentle waif seeking her way through the night into womanhood, and that of a coachman seeking to claim the knowledge of her heart.

This is about the nature of dreams brought from night to day, of courage and wit, and of lands long lost. Among rangers it has become a new myth about the quest to reclaim sacred journeys, within and without. Forged within the dream of Britain, this, ladies and gentlemen—my fellow travelers—is a true story. Like any dream, it is a way to learn of the seen and unseen forces of this world. For we carry with us many kinds of dreams: those of ourselves, our families, our native lands, our quests, as well as the dreams of others—and those of other worlds.

Upon learning from the coachman that Vixen Tor was but a short distance away, the ranger knew he had to visit. Formed by the earth itself, tors were often thought to harbor strong magic, Vixen Tor being no exception. The legends of the Vixen were strong, the tales were many. In his efforts to restore the crown, the ranger had traveled to many lands, visiting many races of people, always trying to inform, intrigue, cajole stories, myths, and legends into reality. And here was a legend waiting to be lived, again.

So he hired the coachman, asking only that she deliver him directly, but without undue haste, to the Vixen's keep. Although a female coachman was more than a mere curiosity, she seemed capable. It was for this reason, and this reason alone, that he was willing to risk the journey with her.

A waif, small in size and large in heart, asked to join them. Neither the ranger nor the coachman refused. There was no sense of dread surrounding the simple request. Still, he did not like the feelings brought about by the other half-dozen or so who wished to travel with them. Too many people would make things a bit too clumsy.

Their journey crossed the moors, magical fern-laden lands speckled by grazing sheep.

Gently sloping, rolling hills eased their tension, eased their minds of what might lie before them. As in any good dream, the air was laden with an elixir for the senses, with an awareness that circled about, ready to connect with the feelings of any creature who simply took care to notice.

Directing the carriage this way and that, the coachman evaded the followers seeking the ranger's company, for they knew bits and pieces of his quest, and sought in some way to reclaim the crown themselves. But the ranger was keen on his scouting mission and the coachman, sensing this, adeptly backtracked over the roads she traveled and so dispelled the image of their line of travel.

The main road then veered away into the night, the fog and rain reclaiming it as its own.

This left them on a narrow, seldom-used trail ... all to the ranger's liking.

This sliver of a trail cut abruptly to the right, leaving the small band of travelers at the beginning of the path into the Vixen's most private domain. They eased out of their carriage, stretched, looked around, then continued their journey on foot.

Surprisingly, a large stone on the left shone with a visage and the energy of King Arthur. The ranger then knew that all of this land, including that of the Vixen, was of the crown—an auspicious omen—a message from the crown itself. He trusted this connection with the most high, a domain above human concerns, above the trials of earthly travel. He also knew he must remain couched in respect, for their journey was about to enter the un-known, into lands that lived only in ancient tales told over ample mugs of mead. He was at once anxious, intrigued, humbled, and keenly aware.

In the distance he saw a line of tall trees, showing their strength through the rain, through the last light of day. The coachman, who had traveled this region once before, told the ranger that no, those were not trees. They were, in fact, the line of Vixen Tor. "A clever disguise," mused the ranger, his full instincts now on alert. His appreciation of the Vixen rose within his heart not unlike the illusion rising before him through the haze.

As if to signal this reality, the path quickly became jagged and rugged, stones littering the path to keep the timid away.

Few words were spoken, for they walked quietly, almost tenderly, as they were filled with awe, wonder, excitement—and more than a hint of fear. On the verge of reaching her keep, marked by a craggy stone wall nearly two meters high, a blackbird darted from a nearby tree. It flew in a straight line to the Vixen, her messenger performing its task well. The ranger knew that they had lost any element of stealth and surprise.

As the three stepped closer to her domain, the Vixen changed. Out of the fog and shadows rose tall, jagged rocks that contained a wicked, mighty energy. She was a temptress, a conjuror, a mother of sorceresses openly displaying her power.

Part of worlds never to be touched by humans, she was not evil, although that feeling was thick in the air; she was only herself, with her own ways in this and other worlds. And she would never reveal her true self but to those she chose, and to those she gave just a hint of respect. Part of this bargain, however, was being fully subjected to her ways.

Few lived to tell their stories of meeting the Vixen. Her legacy of myths was cluttered with stories of broken limbs and hearts, pitiful reflections of those who had sought to tame her. As if to accent this point, a goat with broken foreleg hobbled away from the three, not making a sound—an omen reflecting this land, to be sure.

The ranger knew King Arthur had respected Vixen Tor, even had considered her an important part of the crown. Legend had it that after his passing, she banished herself to the center of the moors, cloaking herself in longing for the one who understood, avoiding the passing of mere mortals, and keeping them at bay by entangling them in her magic.

The ranger parted with the others to track out a sure path, his mind unrelenting, as he was set on learning the lesson of the Vixen's dream. The coachman, knowing of a ranger's training, gave way to his instinct. The waif, ever fearful of the unknown, steadfastly inched her way forward while remaining a good distance behind her companions.

Stepping mindfully on rocks to pass over a small river, the ranger then passed through the Vixen's open, weathered, wooden gate. The outer edge of the gate rested on the ground, the other end barely hinged to a wooden post.

He allowed his steps to be guided by flashes of light from the dirt and rocks, a simple trick Merlin had passed on to him.

Immediately upon stepping through the  gate, a black beast appeared. The ranger stood silently, attentively watching and assessing this guardian. The beast's broad head turned to the ranger, its ears flickering while trying to apprise itself of the presence. Its rain-soaked, furry body remained abreast of the path, firmly blocking the ranger's advance.

He stood motionless. Heeding a quiet, deep, inner voice, he knew he should use his feelings to ask the beast to move on. He was here to learn of Vixen Tor and her place within freedom's dream. Their energies mingled, duly assessing one another. He was neither predator nor prey. But he was unsure of the beast's intentions. He neither gave way nor tried to advance. The dream before them spun anew, coming to life from the dreams of each: a dance of unseen forces shaping their worlds.

The beast then shifted, slowly giving ground to the ranger. Although respectful, the ranger grew wary, ever cautious of the distorted feelings about him.

As though out of thin air, the coachman appeared next to him, then just as quickly departed as she sought a trail with better footing on the far side of the hill. The waif remained behind them, near the gate, filled with fearful wonder. Even so, she was able to keep her attention on the ranger and coachman, eager to participate in some small way in this adventure.

The ranger felt that the coachman could fend for herself. Looking a bit nervous, she was up to her ears in something, which was probably hers alone to figure out. With the waif remaining behind, he felt more at ease to continue his quest.

Directly in his path was a huge rock that created an overhang, a dry spot amidst the sloshy, mushy turf of the hill. A strong sensation throughout his body informed him that he had to pass under it. By not passing under he would

lose his edge, and his instincts would then fail him. He also knew that the magic of this land could make it fall squarely on top of him. As he stepped firmly under the massive rock, the tension mounted and the air became thick with converging energies. Just as quickly the strain eased as he passed fully under, and he felt a noticeable weight removed from his shoulders. Although it was part of a ranger's training to proceed without reservation in the face of fear, he would only later realize that he had passed the Vixen's first test of courage.

Another beastly guardian then appeared before him. It blocked the easy trail to the Vixen's heart on his left, leaving open to his right a steep climb up rocks and moss. He moved in that direction to begin his climb.

The rain had made the rocks slippery and the moss pulled out from the earth with much too much ease, making his footing unsure and his climb treacherous.

With little effort he slipped into his training from Merlin, again using dream images to guide his steps. A flash of light here and a gesture from the rocks there. Over the years this had become a matter of simple navigation for the ranger. He was not truly a wizard, for wizards journeyed in ways he could not yet; but, yes, he had learned some magic from the great wizard of King Arthur's court. Even in the dead of night this bit of dream-tracking, as he liked to called it, always guided his steps surely, steadfastly. From tests of time, he had grown to trust it completely.

Suddenly his footing gave way, and to his horror he nearly plunged to the rocks below, a sure fall to his death. As he slipped, his world turned to slow motion; he saw a root jutting out from the wet ground. In one deft motion, he grabbed it and so managed to save himself. Then just as quickly, his instincts told him the Vixen was turning his own dream against him. She was controlling his magic, his destiny. Hers was the greater power in this other-world, and he had better acknowledge this. At the same time, he remained attentive to his task, letting all the energies between them move about gracefully and lightly on the surface of his awareness while allowing his attention to continue engaging and tracking the Vixen's energies. Doing so, he became at once part wizard, part knight: the true mark of a ranger.

Falling back on his early training with the Knights of the Round Table, he withdrew himself a little further from the magic, shifting himself to rely solely on his physical senses. He now grabbed on to tufts of grass and moss, testing his hold not once, but twice and three times before he pulled himself further up the steep, jagged slope. He gradually lifted himself over the rim, onto the plateau of the tor. He had passed the Vixen's first test of wits, and her second test of courage.

Now over the ridge, the ranger entered the heart of her home. He was suddenly engulfed by a flash of fear. A goblin had appeared before him, looming toward him out of the twilight. It must have sensed the ranger was ready to fight, for it quickly disappeared back into the rock from whence it had emerged. Its markings remained on the rock's surface. Mirth flickered on the ranger's lips.

He circled about some small boulders and found a cave. He stepped into it and found that it was warm, dry, peaceful ... too peaceful.

It did not feel like a part of
the surroundings. He could
not even feel the onslaught
of rain. He queried his
heart. Then he knew! It was
a trap! Offering a respite for
complacent travelers, the
cave would ease them to their doom, into deep
sleep or perhaps into the bellies of the beasts
who wandered about the tor. Seemingly in one
step, he moved quickly back into the cold, a
single act of will and determination. He had
passed the Vixen's second test of wits.

Looking up, he saw her face brooding over
him. Perhaps chiseled into the rock by the
forces of nature, or perhaps by her own making,
she loomed above him. At first, she looked

somewhat like an elegant eagle, yet she had two beaks, two tongues. Repelled by the sight, he knew he could never trust her. In the same breath, he now knew her. She carried a treachery unmatched. But as taught by both knight and wizard, he continued to apply no judgment as his was a mission of learning, and for this he must remain objective and not laden with ordinary human concerns.

As he walked in the direction of a more gentle path, which he thought would lead him away from her home, he glanced over his shoulder. He wished to once again glimpse her strange, savage beauty. He found himself holding two opposite thoughts, two opposite images in his mind: "Wicked beauty." Her face turned toward him. "What magic is this?" he wondered, his heart jumping an extra beat.

Sensing another person, he turned abruptly and found himself straight in the path of the coachman. She was a bit dazed, as though her world had turned upside down and were spinning out of control. Feeling as though he had gained what he had sought, the ranger suggested they leave. She agreed. He took care not to close off his awareness of the Vixen. It would still remain a tricky departure.

Walking side by side, they began their departure. Taking only two steps, to the left the ranger noticed a crevice of sorts, a small hollow joining two larger formations of rock. It was sweet, enticing, delicate, yielding, and yet full of the Vixen's terrible energy. He knew it was her essence, carrying a power that turns girls into women and drives men mad. If a woman isn't careful, the power imprisons her, leaving her full of empty power as she loses sense of the higher power of the crown, leaving her to live only within the Vixen's dream. If a man never learns to grow beyond this seduction, he remains forever estranged from his own heart, subject to the whims and the dreams of others. It is a power greater than most mortals can ever bear to witness.

It was then that the ranger decided he would never return. He thought he had learned what he needed to learn, so he began turning his attention to which lands he would soon scout so he might finish his quest. Noticing that he was a bit full of himself, he returned his attention to the moment and aimed himself away from the tor.

Still, he wanted one more look. Turning toward the Vixen, he found that she had turned her head once again and her double beak smiled at him, mocking his lack of understanding.

His ranger's mood returned suddenly, ferociously! He would not allow himself to have a weak relationship with any part of the crown. He would never bow to, or be bowed by, any creature, of this or any other world. Nor would he allow another to bow to him. This manner would be the only way he could learn, then tell others of his missions so that they might catch the mood of what freedom brings.

He then vowed to return, but knew that to do so—to live so that he could return—he must maintain his alertness to the steps that lay before them. Later, in deep reflection, he would work this journey over and over until it was threadbare, reducing his perceptions of it until they were sharp and objective. He would then assess whether his turnabout of decisions arose from his ranger's training, or from an inflated sense of self; the difference between the two often being a matter of life or death in a ranger's world.

Now matching stride with the coachman, he glanced at her and saw that she had been transformed. She told him that through her adventure, she had learned from her heart that she was an  apprentice sorceress, the Vixen had touched her so deeply and so thoroughly. The ranger wondered at what magic was stirring within her.

"I am very much of her," said the coachman to the ranger. "Yet will I have to be like her? She makes you feel free without giving you true freedom."

The ranger acknowledged the Vixen side of the coachman. But he also knew the goodness in her heart, their separate dreams had mixed long enough for him to see fully through her.

"The Vixen is a dream within us all," he replied, "but the greater magic of the crown will always guide your steps."

Accepting the ranger's prophecy, she relaxed and felt herself come more to life with each passing step.

Noticing that she had quickly become ready for the next instruction, the ranger added, "Find the core of spirit within and you will have taken a step to restore the crown of the land. The crown, you see, is also a dream within us all. We have simply let other dreams command our attention, so the crown has

become something barely noticeable by most."
Feeling the truth of his words, the coachman
sighed heavily.

They departed the top of the tor, amazed,
bewildered, and thankful for their lessons. A
keen vigor surged through their veins.

On the bottom of the slope, they reunited
with the waif and all began the walk out of the
Vixen's land. The coachman, having completely
accepted her fate, was continuing to come to
life in a new way. The waif was busy placing
one foot in front of the other. The ranger
began to feel transported beyond this adventure into dreams yet waiting.

As they walked, the ranger gently coaxed
the waif as a father would his daughter. He
didn't hasten her, because she might fall into

the water, or crash into the soggy turf. He simply sent her strong feelings of clarity and surefootedness, leaving her to figure out her path. Testing, moving, and retreating through the invisible maze, the waif crisscrossed the stream that flowed just outside the wooden gate.

As the waif found the path away from the tor, the ranger and coachman stepped up their pace, yet continued to walk carefully, not to make a mess of the land. They stopped now and then so the waif could catch up. While they waited, the two compared notes on how to find a sure path away from the tor. As soon as the waif came into view, they were off again.

Although she was deeply troubled by the Vixen, the waif stayed alert, and while never fully advancing, never once retreated. Indeed, it was she who pointed out poison mushrooms growing along their path, a reminder to the coachman and the ranger of the nature of this land. "The waif has mettle," he thought to himself, a character deep within that waited to grow stronger with the passing days, something that would allow her to one day engage her own adventures.

Stopping, then turning back toward the tor, they found the Vixen had again cloaked herself. Simple, raw power emanated from the land, through the rocks, into the heavens. Yet she was a bit more gentle now, with no trace of treachery. A golden toad hopped across the path in front of them and disappeared into the fern.

At the end of the trail that marked the outer edges of the Vixen's territory, they

 found a rock set deep within the earth, and dead in the center of the path. It was in the shape of a heart. The ranger turned back his gaze once more, for he could not completely comprehend the meaning, it came as such a jolt. But by now the Vixen had slipped quietly and completely into the night, no trace of her remaining.

The ranger banished from his thoughts all considerations about what might belong to the crown and what might not, now knowing that what might be seen as evil may not really be. It just was, and it had its place. It was the power of dreams, to be used for good or ill.

Still not caring to share the story of her

transformation with the others, the coachman had awakened to her heart. Once jittery with doubt, her stride was now sure. Never again to fear what strangers might say about her, she set upon her own journey of learning and discovery, soon to embark on her own path to restore the crown.

She had learned that the Vixen entices people to arrange their dreams for themselves, and not to strengthen their connection with pure freedom. "Perhaps people needed to know this lesson to hold their own in this world," she thought. But she also knew that it is vital to learn the proper use of this energy, this manner of dream. In days yet to come, it would be the greater learning of this lesson that would guide her steps deeper into sorcery, and through that journey deeper into freedom.

The waif, filled with the others' daring, walked stronger—in fact, a bit stronger than she should. But all the while she kept trying, trying to find her place in this strange world.

Each had gained from the moment, and

each had lost a part of the past. They did not yet fully know, yet each did sense, that they had moved closer to the crown. And each understood well that forevermore the dream of Vixen Tor would remain alive within their hearts and minds.

Dragon
He comes through the mist
with water dripping down.
His scaly body slops mightily on the ground.
He lifts himself into the air and flies in
the spirit sky.
He looks around the magical place.
He races birds like a thunder bolt.
He beds down in his misty cave,
and rests.

The Dream of Vixen Tor is a true story. It occurred during the fall of 1999 while I was presenting a workshop in the magical moors of southern England. We were housed at Grimstone Manor, owned and managed by a community of people seeking to live a more spiritual life. The manor is located very near Dartmoor, in the county of Devon. Except for the placement of the story in time, all the events are exactly as they happened—rather, exactly as I experienced them. Yet even the time period of the story was inspired by my seeing and feeling the energy of a large rock, which I perceived as the spirit of King Arthur. To my reckoning, this makes it a true story. For what is real, anyway?

Interpretations of reality originate from the prevailing models of what people hold to be true. People have experiences, then make sense of them by making them fit with their agreements. These agreements form the glue that holds all the elements of a model together. The model then becomes reality, itself, rather than a tool to approach and use reality. As a result, we confine ourselves to a very limited dream, indeed.

This finding of fact, this discovery of what is true, is governed by considerations of what we think is true. Interpretations stem from what is being lived; they are the subjective experience of physical events. If enough people agree on how those subjective experiences should be interpreted, then we have what is known as objectivity. There is great power in this, as objectivity enables us to build the elements of our world, constructing such things as buildings, roads, and airplanes. At the same time, objectivity diminishes our thirst for what lies ahead, as we cut ourselves off from the value of forging our way into uncharted territories; in other terms, we cut ourselves off from the value of dreaming. By gluing ourselves to the thoughts that allow us to build our world, we inadvertently work at disallowing the magic of our dreams—avenues that enable us to build new constructions—wherever, and however, they occur.

The findings of Copernicus, followed by the evidence of Galileo, turned the world on its ear. The voyages of Columbus and other explorers did the same. So why should we not expect our perception of the world to keep turning into a greater version of what came before?

Some years ago, a new picture of the world was given to us through the teachings of modern Toltecs. According to the works of Carlos Castaneda (perhaps the Copernicus of our time), Toltec philosophy emerged from central Mexico. Based on my travels, I have found that it is gaining worldwide recognition as a viable option to account for how perception works. A principal feature of these teachings is that perception occurs through the interaction of internal and external energy fields. How you manage your internal energy determines anything and everything that you perceive; that is, it determines what you connect with and, therefore, perceive.

My adventure at Vixen Tor was an effect of having been a practitioner of Toltec arts and crafts for thirty years now. It was also influenced by my soon-to-be-born daughter, Emma, as well as the participants of the workshop. Connecting with Emma through dreaming-awake, for instance, took me to potential energy, to the abstract, meaning that I became removed from a concrete, fixed way of perceiving the world. My internal energy then became freer and more fluid, and thereby more capable of interacting with external, or environmental, energy in a different way.

I think that my internal energy field elevated into heightened awareness due to my keen desire to spend time with Emma. As we were separated by physical distance, the only way I could be with her was through shifting my relation with the world and entering a dreaming state while remaining awake, a standard Toltec practice. The workshop participants, in turn, kept me working to remain at that level in order to present the workshop, which dealt with heightened awareness.

In addition, my arrival at Vixen Tor seemed a bit orchestrated by a force beyond human contrivance. The prior year I had made plans to visit the tor, which is a natural rock formation on top of a hill. Everyone in the workshop wanted to experience Vixen Tor, as it was deemed to be the female-energy counterpart of the male-energy tor we hiked to every afternoon. As it was somewhat of a distance away, we all piled into automobiles for the sojourn. But the automobile I was in became separated from the rest of the convoy. My group ended up heading in a different direction; we found ourselves at St. Michael's Church, also on top of a hill. It was there that we felt the "Dragon's Breath," the energy of the wind that travels through the rock walls of the church. The Dragon's Breath is so notice-able it is part of the everyday legend of St.

Michael's. The church itself is remarkable in that while it has no heating it stays warm inside—even when a cold, wet wind blows outside. At any rate, the trip to Vixen Tor never materialized ... that year.

Upon my arrival the following year, the manor we had been using for several years to hold workshops seemed a bit odd to me. Maybe it was simply that I felt off center. Trying to settle down, I walked about the large front yard. Looking off to my left, a row of bushes and small trees suddenly seemed to be the queen and her court. One tree even looked like an illustration on the back of an English pound coin. Then the outlying trees assumed the emotional manner of wizards and knights. They simply felt that way, and seemed to present themselves to the world as such. After all, I was now in Albion, the very land of King Arthur and his trusted adviser, Merlin.

Furthermore, a large, round bush in the middle of the lawn held within it the image of a fetus. No matter what time of day, no matter what patterns formed from the surrounding shadows that were always shifting due to the movement of the sun, the image remained. From this, I felt Emma with me. In fact, time and again during the week, I knew that Emma and I ventured into the abstract together, into rarefied aspects of dreaming. For me, dreaming-awake was the vehicle to do so; as for Emma, I could only wonder at what might be the greater reality of her world (and still do).

I let all of these impressions be, neither trying to uphold the fantasy nor trying to make it into something more of the same. It turned out, however, that this magic of the land set the tone for the workshop.

In short order, the theme of the workshop spontaneously emerged as "restoring the crown," which carries an obvious connotation of English royalty. For the workshop, it took on the meaning of regaining one's center of awareness, one's immediate connection with God. You might also think of this as cultivating Christ consciousness, stimulating the entire kundalini tract, or getting in touch with the core of your being, whichever perspective works for you.

The notion of restoring the crown took full
root during an outing to Plymouth, where our
troupe took on individual disguises for the
afternoon. A computer programmer became a
full-fledged beggar, for instance, or a mild-
mannered accountant became a rogue. The
point of the exercise was to discover the
relativity of how we see ourselves in daily life.
While walking about the very city where the
Pilgrims had departed to their new world, I
came upon a large, green lawn that had an
obelisk in plain view. On the roughly ten-foot-
high cement structure was chiseled a crown. In
a flash of intuition, the obelisk represented the
core of awareness, and the crown represented

elevating this awareness to its highest state. Dreaming-awake, a principal exercise of the workshop, was then viewed as an avenue of personal awakening in order to restore the crown.

During the workshop, a window of time unexpectedly opened to allow us to again pile into automobiles and drive to the Vixen. Amid fog and rain, several cars left the manor. Only one arrived at the path toward Vixen Tor: the coach that carried the ranger, the coachman, and the waif. We three were left alone with our adventure, to join up with the rest of the participants at the end of the trail that both began and ended *The Dream of Vixen Tor*, for they had arrived later but had never embarked to the Vixen.

You might say that this is all imagination. Well, yes, I agree with you. At the same time, our daily world is upheld by imagination. It's all a matter of us agreeing which of our imaginings are real. And we have also worked very hard to squelch the capacities of imagination so that we may feel comfortable within the cloak of social agreements, and social acceptance. Toltecs think that most humans have opiated their imagination, and, as a result, have dulled their sense of allowing reality to continually unfold; indeed, to remain a mystery.

As with my experiences on the manor's front lawn, with Emma, and with the Vixen Tor adventure, the key to allowing reality to unfold is managing how the internal energies of yourself meet, and are influenced by, the external energies of the world. Allowing yourself to let go of a fixed, concrete world enables your internal energies to move about more freely. In so doing, you connect with the world in a different way; in so doing, you allow the perception of new worlds. What kind of dream you live is an adventure uniquely yours. This is the craft of imagination, and the art of exploring perception.

Skillfully practiced, dreaming-awake loosens the reins of perception and lets imagination bear its fruit. If more people make this agreement to live more completely in freedom, we can also retain the positive effects of objectivity. That is, we can all share the quest of restoring the crown, and give way to whatever manner in which such transformation comes. This can be the new agreement of reality, the new objectivity, the new objective.

One of the things I enjoyed most while putting this book together is that it became quite noticeable that the contributors are totally engaged in their quest for freedom. While they may have different definitions, goals, purposes, and ways of getting there, they refuse to be bound by the ordinary.

Moreover, what dreaming-awake means to each of them, and how they use it, demonstrates that this capacity of perception is available to all of us. No matter what age or background, it has many different applications.

✳

An artist and photo-illustrator, Charles Duffie uses dreaming-awake to envision his art, which is necessary for us to capture the vision of the Vixen adventure. As a matter of the publisher's strategy, he was given very little information from which to work. As a result, he had to capture many of his own photos and paint his own images, tapping his imagination, for the disciplined use of imagination is a form of dreaming-awake. The result is an inspired rendering of the Vixen and her ways.

The daughter of a workshop participant, Harriet Louisa Coleman worked in a similar way. She allowed herself to be moved by the story, by the feelings inspired by her native land, and by her desire to write. She says that the characters in Vixen felt like people and creatures from a Celtic time. She could feel their personalities and their energies, which helped her create her poems. This conscious intention, coupled with the ability to allow new things to occur, is a mainstay of dreaming-awake. Young of age, and wise of heart, Harriet's poetry adds even more magic to this book.

And I, too, learned a bit more about the applications of dreaming-awake. By letting the contributors' energies mix with mine, by connecting myself with how I wanted to manage this book, by letting myself move freely about in the book's dream of writing, editing, and production, I was able to glimpse a little more of this eye-opening manner of perceiving the world. In addition, my adventure with the Vixen taught me more about the processes and requirements for entering and maintaining heightened awareness—not to mention that I also had a bit of fun when my reality turned on its ear.

Like the courageous and adventurous explorers before us, and those that are among us now, I invite you to go with your dreams, wherever they occur, and allow them to reveal their stories, so they may give you the time of your life.

It is also with this awareness of how things are, how maybe they aren't, and how maybe they could be, that I invite you to enter—and to live—the journey of the ranger's spirit.

DREAM TRACKING

The Coachman's Journey
Half of me swims under the sea,
and half walks as a spiritual woman.
My golden hair flows from side to side;
my fins glide through the marine-salty water.
One step is a memory,
and the other step is a new journey.
When I go, I hear a hummingbird
reminding me of a dream:
My friends were fish;
my world was blue.
Now I'm astonished,
I can remember all these moments.

Tracking dreams is the skill of entering and stabilizing your dream life. In other words, you wake up inside your dreams. This applies to whether they are of the night or of the day, and whether you are asleep or wide awake. As dream research indicates, our dreams are reflections of ourselves. The people, symbols, or events within a dream often carry meaning; it's only a matter of being able to interpret what is occurring. In this light, tracking your dreams is learning to track the hidden knowledge within yourself.

For instance, while all three of our story's travelers are individuals, I'm sure you can recognize that, at some level, the three travelers are one; and you can probably see these different aspects within yourself as they represent different stages of growth, evolution, and maturity.

The waif is the uncertain child, yearning to know more, desiring to be free, not yet fully capable of action. The coachman is the somewhat more mature person who, after searching for a release from the mundane, finds his or her heart and, in so doing, finds his or her path in life. The ranger is the actualized person, or at least the person who has matured sufficiently to be able to walk a path leading to actualization.

In addition, we can most likely see ourselves and others in the Vixen, her messenger, King Arthur's spirit, and in the other elements of the story. As a result, we can recognize ourselves within and throughout the entire story. This notion of oneness—of being part of everything—is a central component of many of the world's spiritual traditions. Indeed, a core component of heightened awareness is being able to perceive yourself as one with your world. Dreaming, especially dreaming-awake, is an exercise to begin this quest, as is seeing, or gaining an immediate *knowing* about your circumstances. Keep in mind this immediacy of knowing is direct, and therefore transcends reason as a means of understanding our world, as reason works from subject-object relations, from a separation among things.

For Toltecs, part of this knowing is recognizing that the world is made up of energy. And yet this awareness is certainly not limited to Toltecs, for there is growing awareness that the world is composed of energy. As evidenced by the increasing number of lay books on quantum physics—of which energy is a main aspect—that subject is gaining popularity. As a result, a reality in which the world is seen as energy is catching on.

Since the world is made of energy, so, too, are humans. From a Toltec perspective, humans have two energy fields, two bodies: the physical and the nonphysical. Together they comprise the human being. Think of an incandescent light bulb. The filament represents the physical energy field, and the glass represents the outer edge of the nonphysical energy field. Combined, the two fields make up the energy body. What is often called the *aura,* for instance, is not the energy body. It is the energy generated by, and emanating from, the entire energy body. You are more than your physical senses, as wonderful as they might be. And, as wonderful as these senses might be, there is a heck of a lot more waiting to be explored and used. Dreaming-awake is your launch pad.

The capacities of dreaming and seeing result from a person having gained balance between the two energy fields, then having gained a degree of harmony between the personal self and the world. At the same time, dreaming and seeing help generate balance and harmony. So, you see, cause and effect cut both ways. In a world of oneness you have more options than are given in a linear, three-dimensional world. If this is difficult to grasp, don't worry. You really can't understand anyway until you've been there. Let's get to it, then, so you can have your own magical journeys.

Preparation for Dreaming-Awake

In the Flow. To warm up, stimulate your feelings a bit.

1. Relax.

2. Rest comfortably with your eyes closed.

3. Let your feelings flow without censorship. Entertain them without holding on to them or pushing them away. Experience any and all of them.

4. Sink deep into yourself, into your internal world.

5. Gently push your energy out. Reach out and attend to your external world while you're resting with your eyes shut.

6. Try to combine all these steps. In other words, pay complete attention.

7. Pay attention to what is happening *now*.

Gazing and Seeing. As another warmup for dreaming, practice gazing and a hint of seeing.

1. Relax. Try to be nonattached to anything you perceive. In other words, let go and begin to feel a flow of energy.

2. Establish your intent to gaze. Summon your reserves and focus on shifting your perception.

3. Don't focus on the world as you normally might. Don't, for example, pick out an object then look at it. Let your eyes go soft, unfocused.

4. Feel your body merge with the world. Remain centered within your body as you connect with the external world.

5. If you see a haze of light, a thin film of energy, or what looks like swirling dots, let them be. Don't focus on them or you'll kick in your old intent and will refocus automatically on the ordinary, physical world. The light is the nonphysical world breaking into your awareness, and is seeing, proper. Later, when you gain more experience, you will be able to focus on that energy and it

won't disappear. But until you train your eyes, and your body, your normal habits of perception will rule.

6. The more you practice, the more you'll see different things, like the spirit of King Arthur emanating from a rock! Or the aura of a tree. Or the energy body of another person. Or....

Focus on Dreaming

With a bit of care, attention, and practice you can turn your perception of your daily world into a dream. You may also use this awareness to learn how to actually enter the world of ordinary nighttime dreaming; rather, turn ordinary dreaming into something magical and alive. Preliminary exercises follow.

Entering Your Dreams

1. Relax.

2. Develop your purpose(s) for entering your dreams.

3. Relax some more. Build your thoughts toward dreaming from inner relaxation, not an outer hardness of "I must do this."

4. Take a nap.

5. Intent is the vehicle, movement, or tunnel that brings about conscious dreaming. To arrive at your intent, gather the feelings associated with practicing with nonphysical energies (such as those given above), aim these toward entering your dream world, then isolate the very personal feeling that arises from this quest. This is the hook to remember your intent.

Nova

1. Extend two beams of light energy outward and perpendicular to each side of your physical body: one beam out of the right side, one beam out of the left side.

2. Retract these energies to a specific location inside your chest. Your breath may help you build these energies. For example, exhale as you extend the light, inhale as you retract the light.

3. Again extend two beams of light energy from your body. This time extend one out of the top of your head and one out of the bottoms of your feet.

4. Retract these energies to the same location as in step 2.

5. Form the energy within your chest into a sphere (or other form natural to yourself, such as another geometric form or that of an animal), then gently project it away from your physical body.

Too Tired? When you're too tired to do any exercise, that may be the time to push forward. But you don't have to make yourself miserable, either. Try this one when you are just too tired.

1. Allow your fatigue to saturate your physical body. This facilitates relaxation and the notion that it is okay to be fatigued. (This also feeds over into actual dreaming as you

learn to deal with the unexpected. Stay relaxed; it's okay.)

2. Perceive a hollow core at the center of your physical body.

3. From that core, push or expand the fatigue energy outward in all ways, in all directions. As you do, the core of the energy also expands.

4. Contract that energy. The core of the energy will contract as well. Again, your breath may facilitate your experience. Exhale as you expand the energy away from you, inhale as you retract the energy.

5. As you fall asleep, expand and contract your fatigue energy at your own pace. As you expand and contract the energy, know

within yourself that you are doing so in order to build dreaming intent.

Now that you have buffed up your perception, try a few exercises to help you connect with your path, your external world, your waking dreams.

Dreaming-Awake

Initially, dreams occur as you place your attention on the second energy field. Dreams then shift about—scene to scene, dream to dream—because your attention is not stable. Therefore entering a dream is one skill, stabilizing it is another.

With practice, the first and second fields merge, elevating your daily life into a dream, and making your dreaming more usable and practical. You're also more in the here and now, perhaps the most practical feature of all.

Tracking Dreams

1. Relax. (Sense a pattern?)

2. Walk about slowly. Anywhere will do.

3. Take it easy. Feel the environment. Feel what's going on inside yourself. *Feel.*

4. Pay attention. (Another pattern?)

5. Feel yourself to be completely a part of your world.

6. Connect the feeling of your "external" dream to a place deep within yourself.

7. Imagine the air is full of viscous energy, awareness itself. Feel around you for peak energies, for energies that have more snap.

8. Expand your feeling so you're aware of as much as possible, simultaneously.

9. Practice walking and talking while performing these exercises. Learn to feel the energy about you. Listen for it with your body. Let it speak to you, and you to it.

Connect with Your Path

1. While in your gazing posture, open yourself to feeling. Then reflect on the following:

2. What makes you love the world? Connect that feeling to a point six inches away from your body.

3. What makes you stronger? Connect that feeling one foot away.

4. What makes you happier? Connect that feeling two feet away.

5. Now extend yourself into your entire world. Into the entire universe.

6. Return to your center, your place of balance within yourself. (If you can't feel it immediately, feel around for it. You know how.)

The Vixen Adventure

1. Stop telling yourself over and over and over what you think and feel the world is. In other words, don't make the world concrete, inflexible, unyielding.

2. Allow yourself to step into new worlds.

3. Know what you want out of life so you can return to this world.

4. Is all of this difficult? Yes, it is. The remedy?

5. Put your mind to the task.

Lessons Learned

Dreaming-awake has unlimited possibilities. What you learn may be similar to, or quite unlike, any other lesson. There are constants, though, and I think the following few lessons are good for anyone, anywhere, to learn.

1. You are responsible for your life, and your world. Live accordingly. (More rules and steps for this? No, you're responsible for you.)

2. Let go from time to time. Let new thoughts and sensations enter your awareness.

3. Don't judge everything, all the time. Let the world breathe. (Remember Lesson 1.)

4. Respect your life, others, and the world ... no matter what world it is.

5. Keep pushing forward on your quest, even when you don't feel like it, and especially when things become difficult. (Laziness has many crevices.)

6. No matter how large or small your resources or your abilities, trust yourself.

7. Be present. The here and now contains the gift of your life.

Summary

I trust you discovered that many of these exercises are very relaxing. A common thread in them is the focus of remaining centered in your body, not in your head. Dreaming-awake requires using the body, not the intellect. Indeed, gazing, feeling, and seeing are all done with the full body. Exercising your awareness generates the momentum to shift how you perceive the world. Since you are using more of your complete resources, you automatically heighten your awareness. With time and tons of practice, there comes a magical day when you are able to enter, and maintain, dreaming-awake.

Practice, then, even when you don't think anything is happening. Don't give up on your quest. At some point, new perceptions will be at your disposal and you will have taken a strong step into the adventure of your life.

Remember, heightened awareness is often called dreaming-awake, as your environment takes on a dreamlike quality. Colors are clearer, sharper. You feel connected. You feel more capable. You feel like you're not at the mercy of the world, and that you can actively shape your dream ... your life.

Waif
A pretty young girl in a four-acre wood,
I imagine I'm in a warm, cozy blanket
with a lively fire opposite me,
going higher and higher.
I'm magic;
I can make lovely Sunday dinners for
    my stomach.
My shelter is a tree;
an oak tree is my special home.
I'm to become the woman inside me,
but I can feel the different ages within me.
I have no friends at all,
and no one knows me.
I run like the wind
in a cold dusky day;
I float in the sky like an eagle,
but land in sudden silence;
then I fall asleep in my tree.

ACKNOWLEDGEMENTS

The Coachman and The Waif
Swish, swosh with the whip;
gallop, gallop the horses go.
Hurry, hurry chuckles waif,
gallop, gallop faster!
You can come on;
come on!
Now we'll be late for our sleeping
    dream at night.
I'm getting tired of this ride.
Come, come now,
I'm flying away.

For adding immense enjoyment to writing *Vixen,* a tip of the hat to the pros, Chuck Duffie and Harriet Coleman; for behind-the-scenes work of Jennifer Dumm, Cynthia Mitchell, and Gail Wiley, thanks again; for their assistance above and beyond the call, thanks to Grace Pedalino, Rebecca Williamson, and Roswitha; and, for their impeccability, special thanks to Simon Buxton, The Sacred Trust, and Emma's companions, the fearless rangers of Grimstone Manor!
Ken Eagle Feather

I would like to thank Alex Hrynash for telling Ken about my poems, because this got the ball rolling. Thanks to my mum, and Wanda, who encourage my writing. A big thanks to Ken Eagle Feather for asking me to write my poems for this book, and becoming part of the Vixen Tor adventure.
Harriet Louisa Coleman

Photography, painting and scans were used to create the illustrations in this book. The cover is based on a photo of Vixen Tor, kindly provided by Jaqui Rigby. Thanks also to Canon, Apple, Adobe, and Corel for the tools to capture and create these images, and to WestStock, PhotoDisc, and Artville for several key photographs. Thanks to Brent and the Sundogs; though I don't miss the six-month winters, I do miss the Fargo community and creative back-and-forth. Thanks to Ken for this story, and the learning journey he led us through while we worked hard to create something good. Thanks to Gabrielle for the wedding remembrance. Thanks to the Duffies and Petersons for taking care of Jen and me. And as always, thanks to Genevieve for taking care of me in ways no one else could comprehend. Charles Duffie

Dream Ranger

I can dream with my eyes open,
and I'll tell you a story about a dream
    I dreamed:
a fox howling above the mountain,
crying for love and sorrow,
gliding through the sky,
calling, calling to me.
I try to catch him with my delicate
    hands,
but off he goes,
off he goes,
away, away.